Abracadabra! You can add a light and happy touch to your child's learning time! *Homework Magic* will help you reinforce important basic phonics skills that will build the foundation for future learning. The one-on-one time you spend teaching your child is an irreplaceable gift that will give him or her the extra knowledge that will lead to self-confident, successful school years.

HOW TO USE THIS BOOK

- Choose a place to work with your child that is comfortable, cozy, and relatively free of distraction. This is special time!

- Remove the "magic wand" from the binding of the book. Tear the perforated lines to create the wand. Set the wand aside until it is time for your child to check his or her answers.

- Make sure your child understands the directions before beginning an activity.

- Invite your child to complete the problems on an activity page in pencil, offering as much help and encouragement as your child needs to feel successful.

- When it is time for your child to check his or her answers, show him or her how to use the wand to reveal the hidden answer. Have fun during this part of your learning time! When your child reveals the correct answer, say *abracadabra!* or *presto!* or *wow!* If your child reveals an answer that differs from his or hers... *Hocus pocus!* Just erase the incorrect answer and rework the problem with your child.

FS111119 Homework Magic—Phonics Review Grade 2
All rights reserved—Printed in the U.S.A.
Copyright © 1999 Frank Schaffer Publications, Inc.
23740 Hawthorne Blvd., Torrance, CA 90505

ISBN #0-76820-433-X

Edited by Cindy Barden
Illustrated by Becky J. Radtke
Cover Design by Good Neighbor Press, Inc.

This book or parts thereof may not be reproduced in any form or mechanically stored in any retrieval system without written permission from the publisher.

Listen to These Sounds
Initial Consonants

Write the letter you hear at the **beginning** of each word.

(fish)	F	(watch)	W
(bat)	B	(question)	Q
(lock)	L	(nail)	N
(mice)	M	(sock)	S
(door)	D	(king)	K

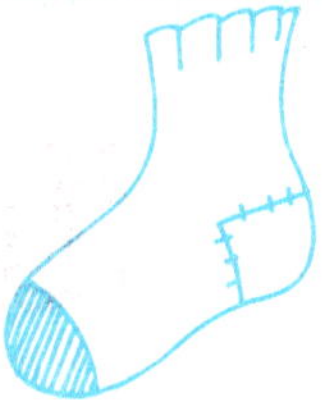

Why don't bears wear shoes and socks?

What's at the Beginning?

Initial Consonants

Write the letter you hear at the **beginning** of each word.

(pig)	P	(sun)	S
(tiger)	T	(goat)	G
(yo-yo)	Y	(pear)	P
(balloon)	B	(jacks)	J
(zipper)	Z	(violin)	V

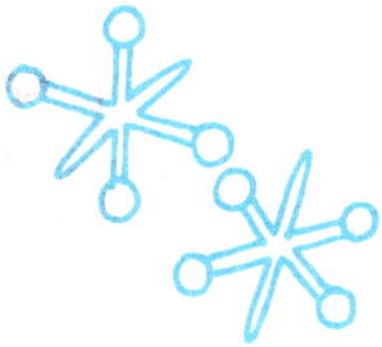

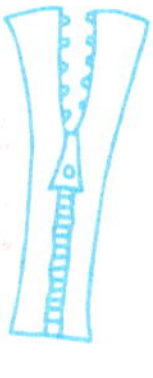

⭐ Which member of Congress wears the largest hat?

The End of the Road
Ending Consonants

Say the name of the picture. Circle the letter you hear at the end of each word.

(g)   b   d

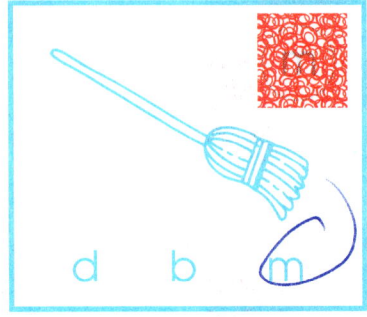

d   b   (m)

j   (r)   k

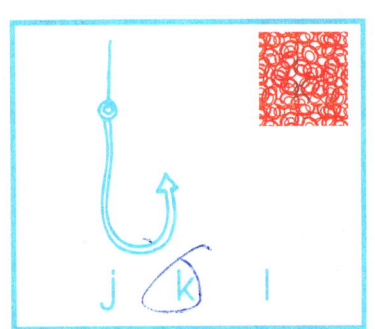

j   (k)   l

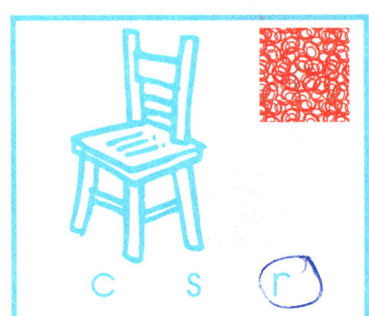

c   s   (r)

s   (r)   c

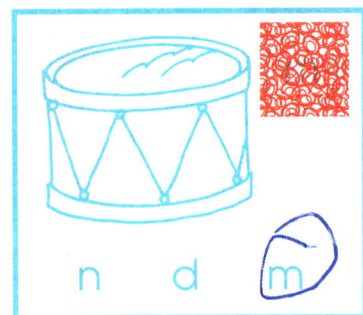

n   d   (m)

(g)   p   q

p   q   (r)

What do baby ghosts wear on their feet?

What's at the End?
Ending Consonants

Write the letter you hear at the end of each word.

What do polar bears wear on their heads?

Let's Do More!
Ending Consonants

Write the letter you hear at the **end** of each word.

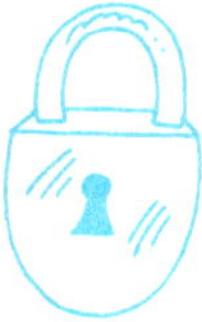

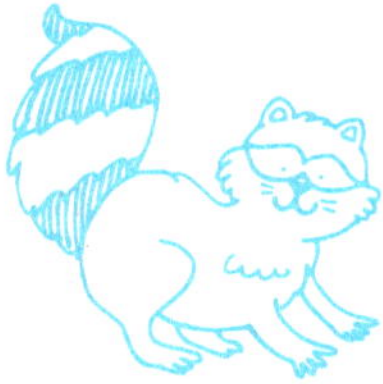

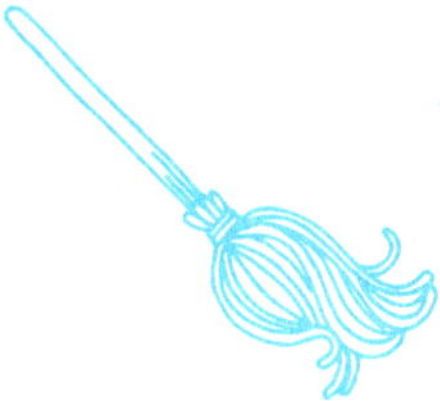

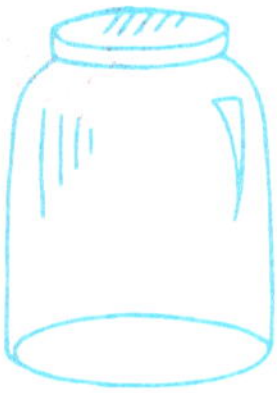

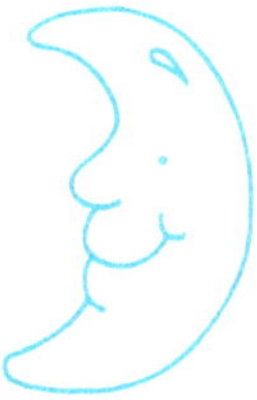

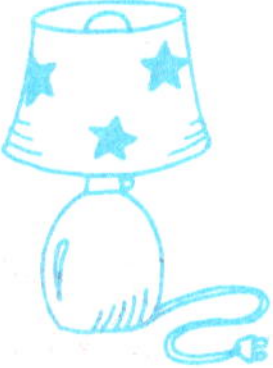

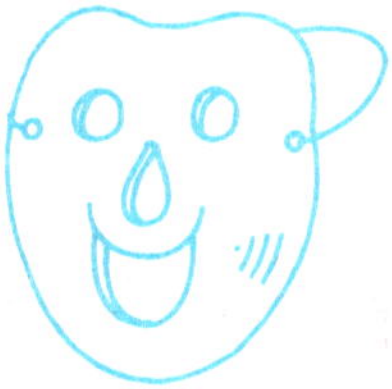

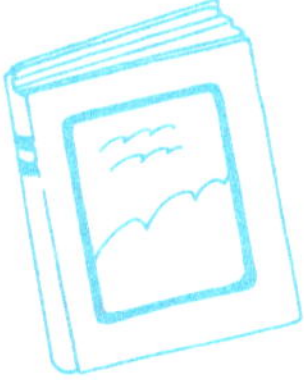

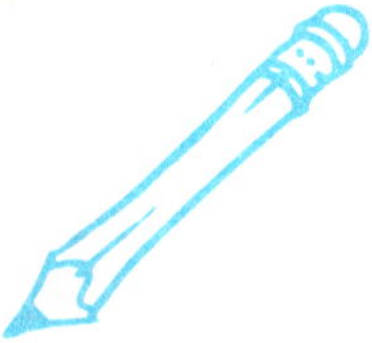

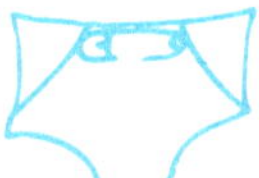

What's long, orange, and wears diapers?

This Is Fun!

Beginning and Ending Consonants

Write the letter you hear at the beginning and end of each word.

___ enci ___   ___ adde ___   ___ ain

___ octo ___   ___ es   ___ oo

___ ame ___   ___ uc ___   ___ oo ___

What animal do most people wear on their heads?

Easy Does It!

Beginning and Ending Consonants

Write the letter you hear at the **beginning and **end** of each word.**

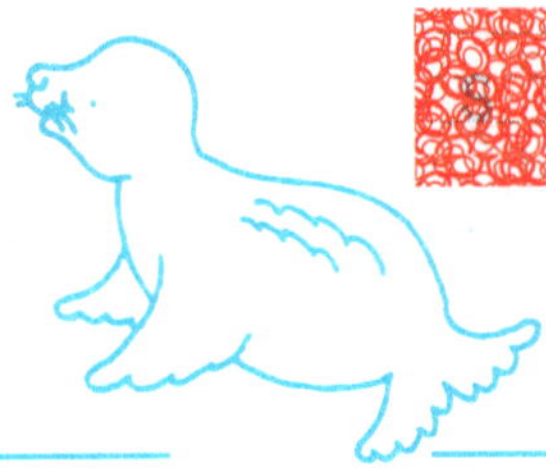

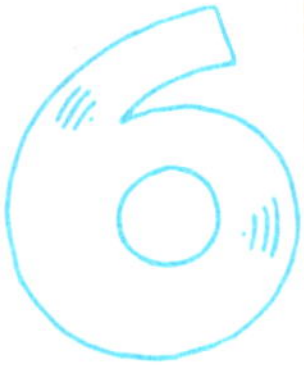

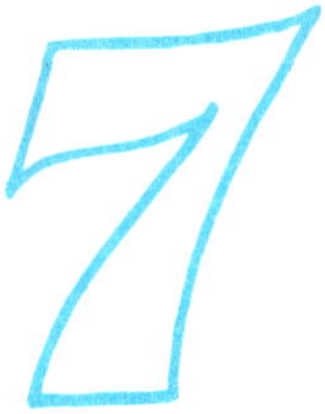

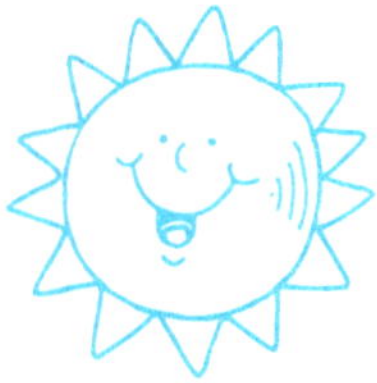

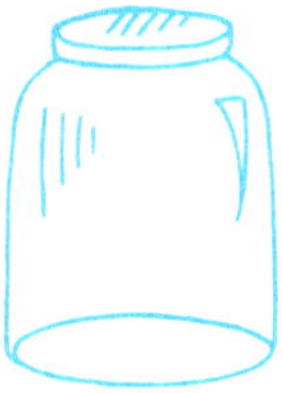

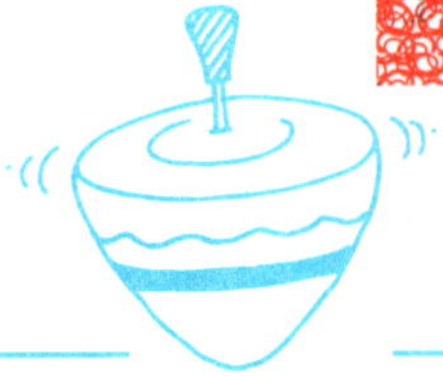

___ e a ___

___ i ___

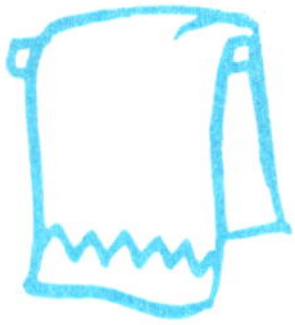

___ e v e ___

___ u ___

___ a ___

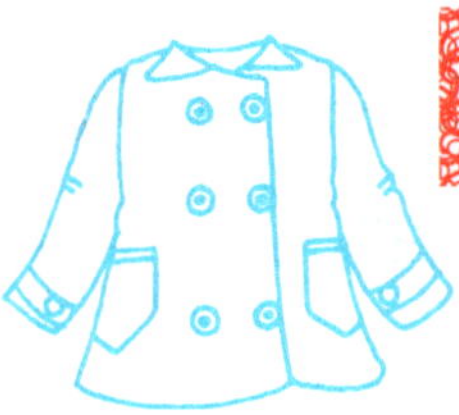

___ o ___

___ o w e ___

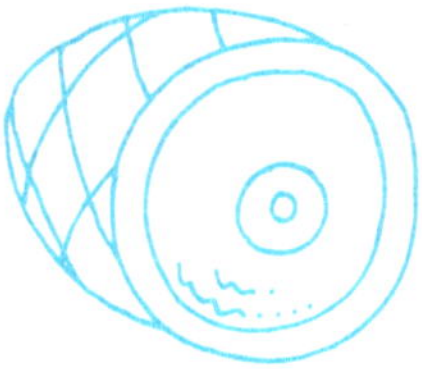

___ a ___

___ o a ___

What animal never has anything to wear?

Let's Write Some Long Vowels

Long Vowels a, e

Say the name of the picture. Print the vowel you hear.

Where do cats hang up their clothes?

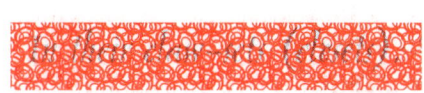 

Totally Nice!

Long Vowels i, o

Say the name of the picture. Print the vowel you hear.

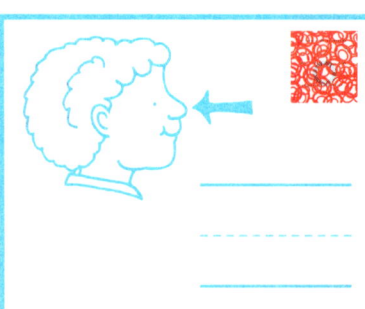

How does a rooster keep his feathers so neat all the time?

Get Your Pencil

Long Vowels i, o, u

Say the name of the picture. Print the vowel you hear.

 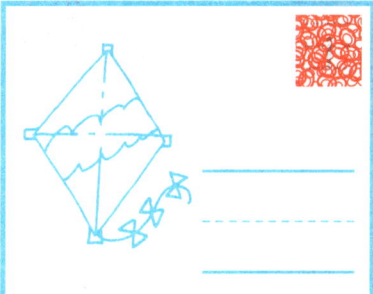 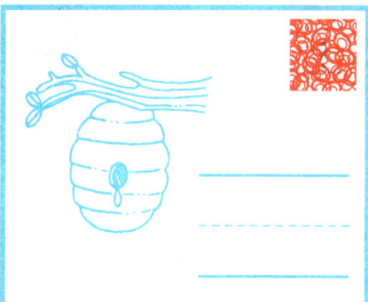

 Where do felines buy their clothes?

You're Swell!
Long Vowels Review

Write the missing long vowel: **a, i, o,** or **u.**

Play	School
sk____te	gl____be
sl____de	c____ge

Animals	Home
____pe	ph____ne
m____le	v____se

What kind of bows are impossible to untie?

What Are These?
Long Vowels Review

Write the missing long vowel a, i, o, or u in the first blank. Write the silent e in the second blank.

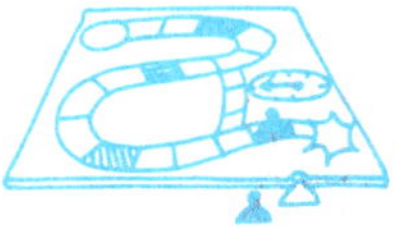

m _ c _

g _ m _

c _ k _

m _ l _

b _ n _

r _ k _

b _ k _

f _ c _

fl _ t _

h _ s _

⭐ What is the hardest key to carry in your pocket?

You Know Your Short Vowels

Short Vowels a, e

Say the name of the picture. Print the vowel you hear.

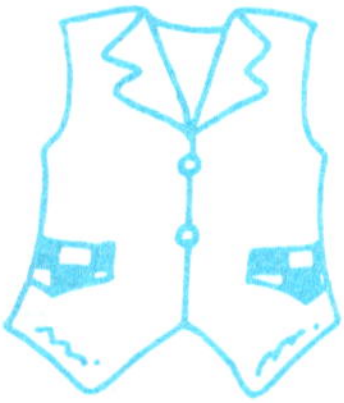

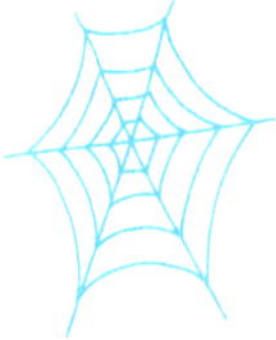

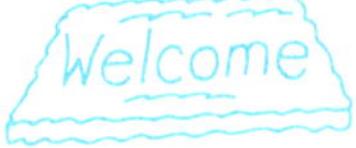

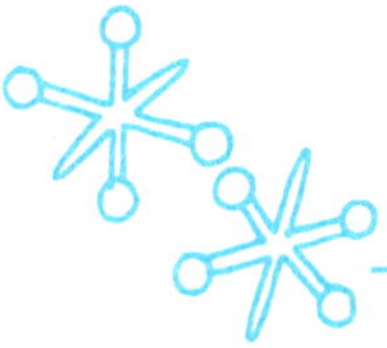

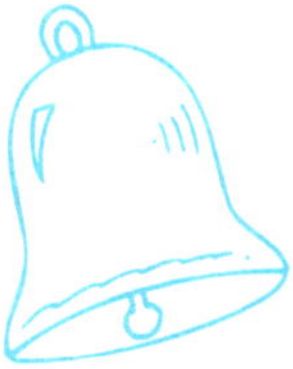

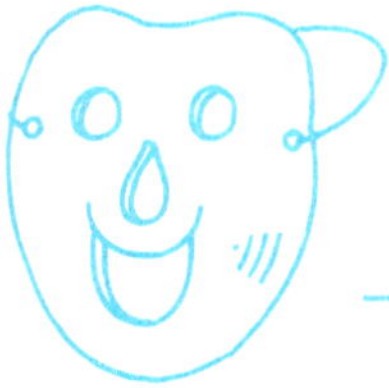

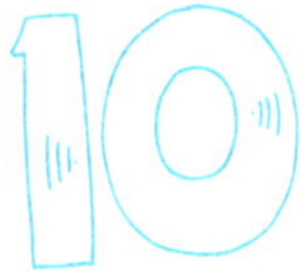

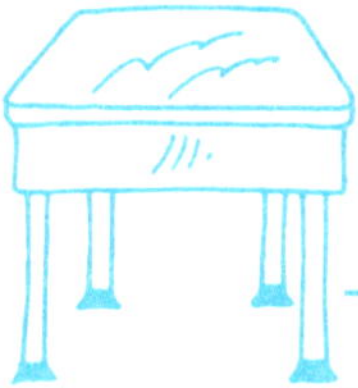

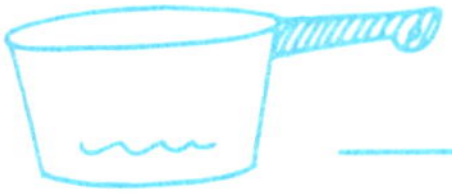

When can your pocket be empty and still have something in it?

You're Fantastic!

Short Vowels a, i

Say the name of the picture. Print the vowel you hear.

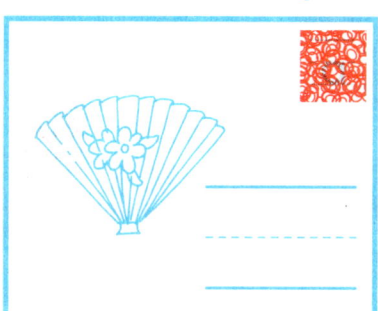

Why is it a good idea to have holes in your jeans?

© Frank Schaffer Publications, Inc.

Lucky Duck!

Short Vowels a, u

Say the name of the picture. Print the vowel you hear.

 What two-word rhyme describes what insects wear?

© Frank Schaffer Publications, Inc.

You'll Like This a Lot!

Short Vowels o, e

Say the name of the picture. Print the vowel you hear.

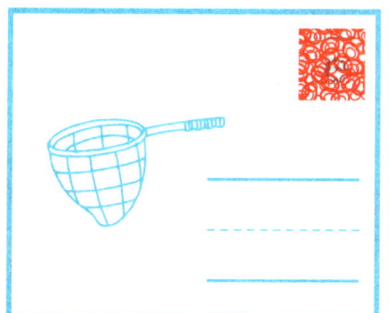 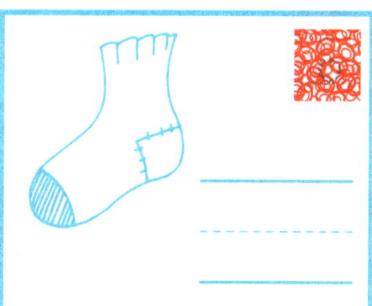 

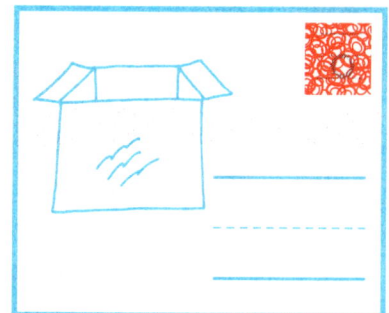  

 What does it mean if you find four horseshoes?

© Frank Schaffer Publications, Inc.   17   FS111119 Phonics Review Grade 2

You're the Best!

Short Vowels Review

Write the missing short vowel: **a**, **e**, **i**, **o**, or **u**.

p __ g   h __ t

c __ p   ch __ ck

n __ st   f __ n

b __ g   m __ p

d __ ck   fr __ g

★ Why do men wear blue suspenders?

This Takes the Cake!

Long/Short Vowel a

Read the words in the triangle. If a word has the sound of long vowel a, write it in the square. If a word has the sound of short vowel a, write it in the circle.

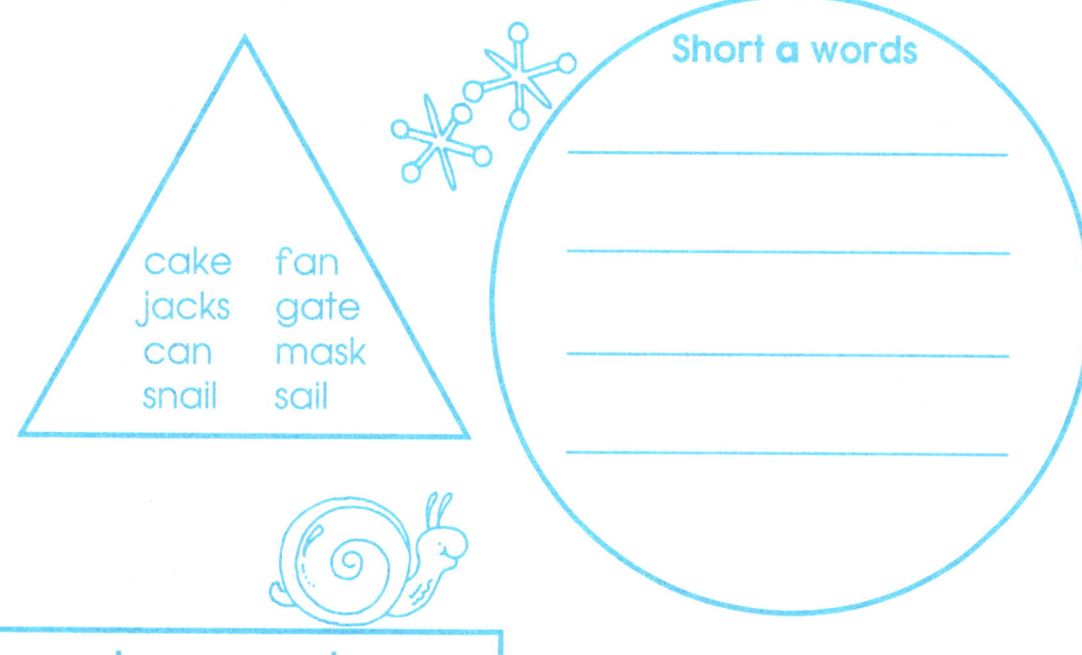

Triangle words: cake, fan, jacks, gate, can, mask, snail, sail

Short a words
_____
_____
_____
_____

Long a words
_____
_____
_____
_____

Short a   Long a

What has teeth but cannot eat?

Big Cheese!

Long/Short Vowel e

Read the words in the octagon. If a word has the sound of long vowel e, write it in the square. If a word has the sound of short vowel e, write it in the circle.

Short e words

knee   seven
net   cheese
seal   jet
bell   leaf

Long e words

Short e   Long e

What is full of holes but holds water?

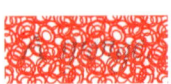

It's Nice!

Long/Short Vowel i

Read the words in the pentagon. If a word has the sound of long vowel i, write it in the square. If a word has the sound of short vowel i, write it in the circle.

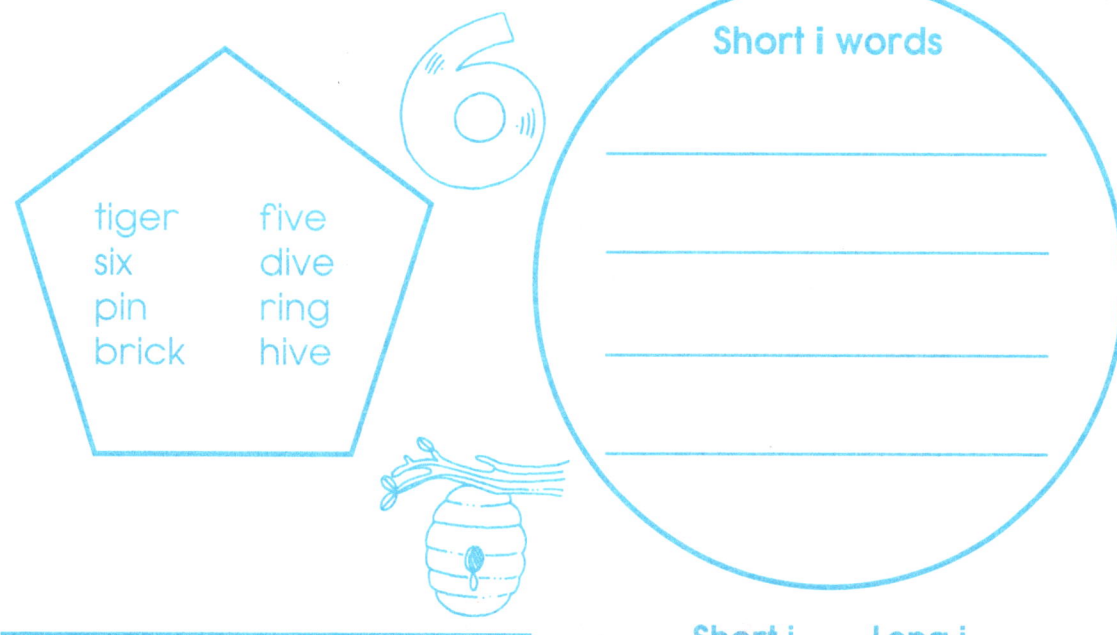

Words in pentagon: tiger, six, pin, brick, five, dive, ring, hive

Short i words

Long i words

Short i   Long i

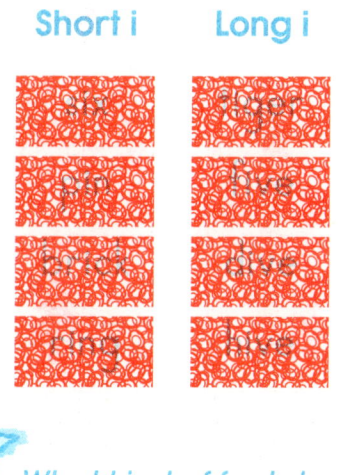

What kind of foot do you find in a book?

Good Job!

Long/Short Vowel o

Read the words in the diamond. If a word has the sound of long vowel **o**, write it in the square. If a word has the sound of short vowel **o**, write it in the circle.

goat   dot
rose   mop
fox   cone
boat   lock

Short o words

Long o words

Short o   **Long o**

⭐ What kind of coat has no buttons and is put on wet?

Huge Hugs!
Long/Short Vowel u

Read the words in the oval. If a word has the sound of long vowel **u**, write it in the square. If a word has the sound of short vowel **u**, write it in the circle.

Short u words

_____

_____

_____

_____

cube   duck
ruler hug
run   bug
flute suit

Long u words

_____

_____

_____

_____

Short u   Long u

What do kangaroos wear?

Let's Review Some Vowels!

Long and Short Vowels

Write the vowels **a, e, i, o,** or **u** to complete each word.

f__sh

st__te

pl__nt

w__b

wh__te

sn__ke

st__nd

p__nd

tre__

h__ge

h__lp

dr__ss

Knock, knock.
Who's there?
Eileen.
Eileen who?

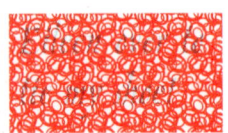

More Review for You!

Long and Short Vowels

Read the words in the cloud. Decide if the word has a short or long vowel. Write the word on the correct pencil.

long vowels

short vowels

cake   hat   pig   mop   mule
hill   tap   be   dime   feet
job   soap   nut   flute

What did the clerk say when Jack asked, "May I try on the pants in the window?"

It Looks Like Rain!

Long Vowels

Match each word to its picture. Underline the two vowels in each word.

pail  goat

boat  rain

fruit  coat

chain  soap

tree  seal

train  tie

Why did the golfer wear two pairs of pants?

26

Don't Be a Lazy Daisy!
Y As a Vowel

Print the answers to the riddles. Use the words in the sock.

twenty   story
happy   money
candy   daisy

I am fun to read.

I am a _____.

I am a sweet treat.

I am _____.

I am good to save.

I am _____.

I am a number.

I am _____.

I am a flower.

I am a _____.

I am not sad.

I am _____.

What two-word rhyme describes what you would use to fix a pair of broken sneakers?

Bravo for Blends!

Consonant Blends bl, br

Write the consonant blend you hear at the beginning of each word.

____ anket

____ ead

____ imp

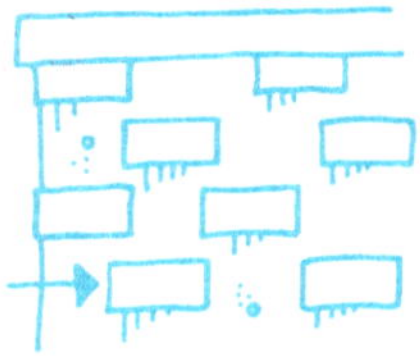

____ ick

____ ock

____ oom

____ ouse

____ ush

What two-word rhyme describes a pair of pants for a thin person?

_____

We're Crazy About Blends

Consonant Blends cl, cr

Write the consonant blend you hear at the **beginning** of each word.

_____ ock	_____ ab	_____ ayon

_____ oud	_____ oss	_____ own

_____ ub	_____ own	

What do you call a person who walks around with a dictionary in the back pocket of his jeans?

Fly, Fly, Away!

Consonant Blends fl, fr

Write the consonant blend you hear at the beginning of each word.

_____ ag

_____ ame

_____ y

_____ ame

_____ ower

_____ og

_____ ute

_____ uit

The more you take, the more you leave behind. What are they?

Beat Your Drum!

Consonant Blends dr, gr, gl

Write the consonant blend you hear at the beginning of each word.

_____ ess

_____ obe

_____ agon

_____ oves

_____ um

_____ apes

Light as a feather, there is nothing in it; yet the strongest man can't hold it for much more than a minute. What is it?

_____ ill

You're a Prize!

Consonant Blends pl, pr

Write the consonant blend you hear at the beginning of each word.

____ ane

____ ice

____ ince

____ um

____ ate

____ ize

____ ant

____ incess

What kind of foot has four legs?

Smile! You're Special!

Consonant Blends sl, sm, sp

Write the consonant blend you hear at the **beginning** of each word.

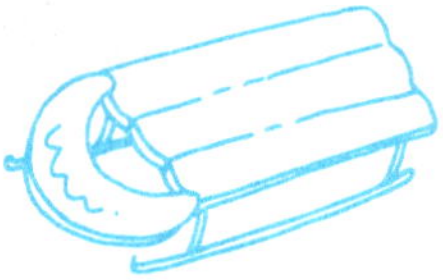

_____ ile	_____ ider	_____ oke
_____ ed	_____ oon	_____ ide
_____ eeve	_____ ipper	

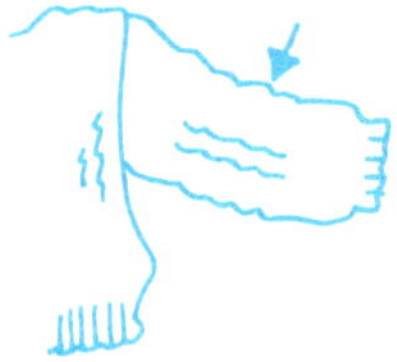

What two-word rhyme describes what a man with purple whiskers has?

Let's Skate!

Consonant Blends sc, sn, sk

Write the consonant blend you hear at the beginning of each word.

_____ ale

_____ ail

_____ irt

_____ arf

_____ ate

_____ ake

_____ arecrow

If you are in a dark room with a candle, a wood stove, a match, and a gas lamp which should you light first?

Super Star!
Consonant Blends st, tr

Write the consonant blend you hear at the beginning of each word.

_____ arfish	_____ ick	_____ ee
_____ iangle	_____ one	_____ ain
Why is the sky so high?	_____ uck	_____ unk

Blend Review

Consonant Blends

Print the answers to the riddles. Use the words in the tag.

treat   clown
frown   brown
smile   please

When people are sad they sometimes _____.

I am a color. I am _____.

I am a frown, upside down. I am a _____.

He makes you laugh. He is a _____.

When you want something, you should say _____.

If you say please, you may get a _____.

What has 100 legs but cannot walk?

R-Blend Festival

Consonant Blends: r blends

Write the consonant blend you hear at the **beginning** of each word.

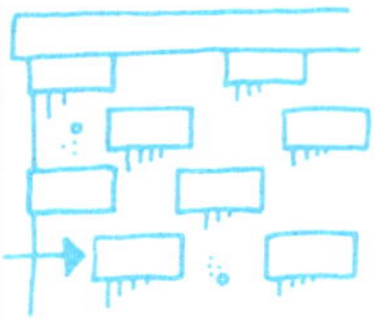

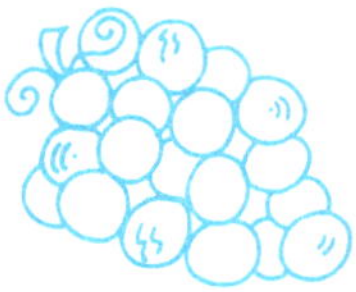

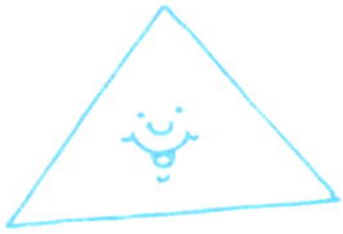

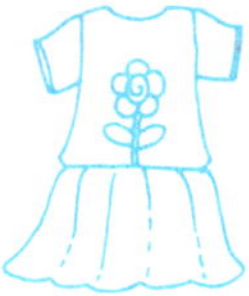

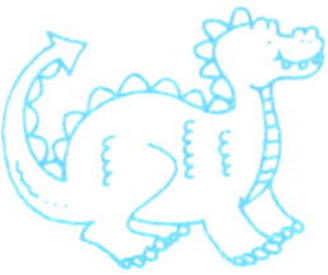

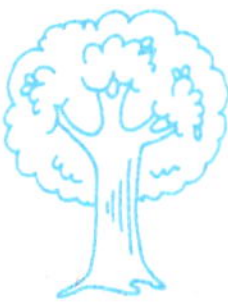

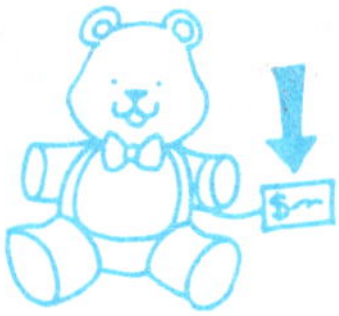

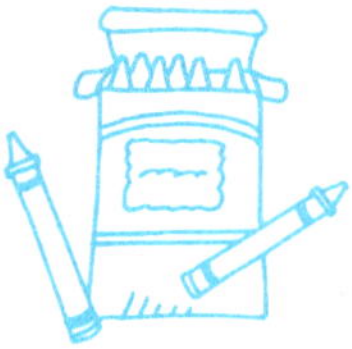

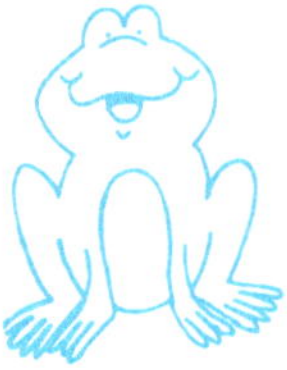

What two-word rhyme describes what a bald hog wears?

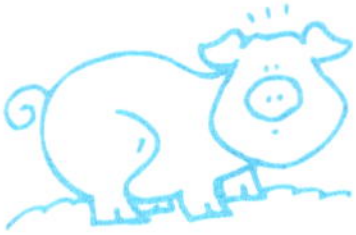

A Little Review for You

Consonant Blends: l blends

Write the consonant blend you hear at the **beginning** of each word.

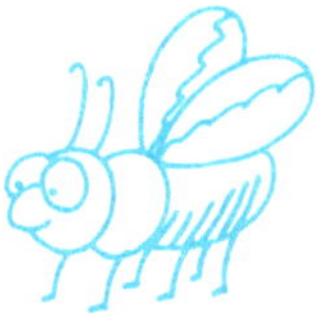

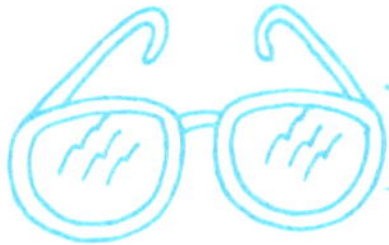

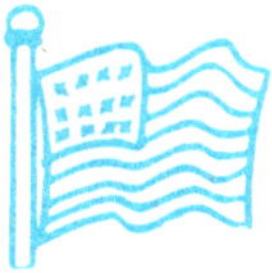

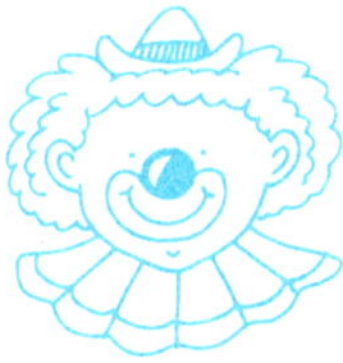

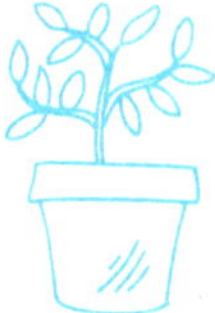

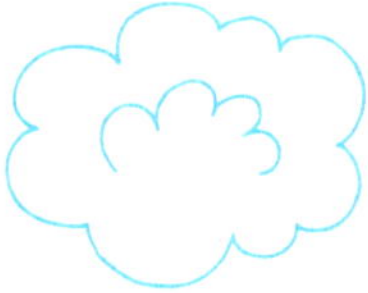

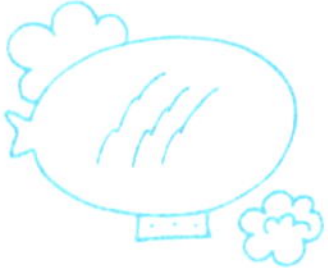

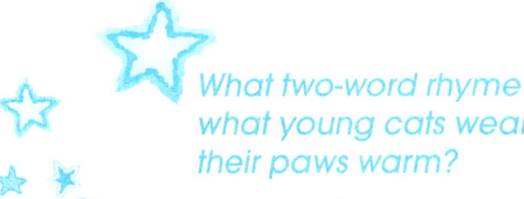
What two-word rhyme describes what young cats wear to keep their paws warm?

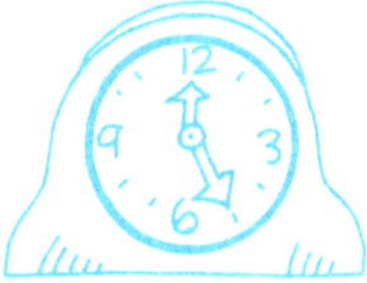

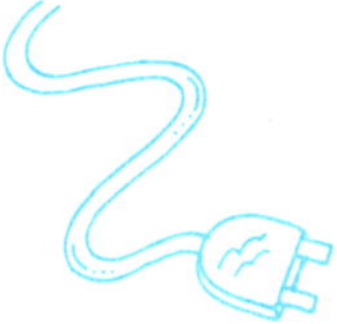

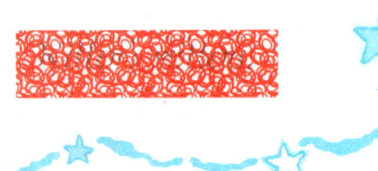

Big Blend Review

Consonant Blends: s blends

Write the consonant blend you hear at the **beginning** of each word.

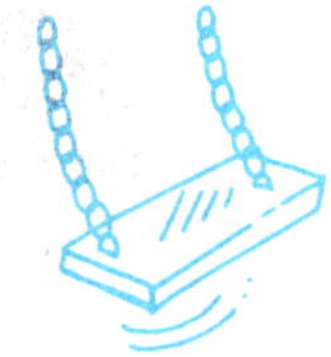

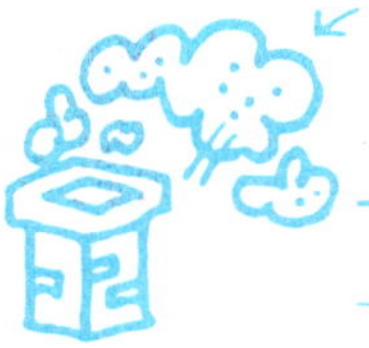

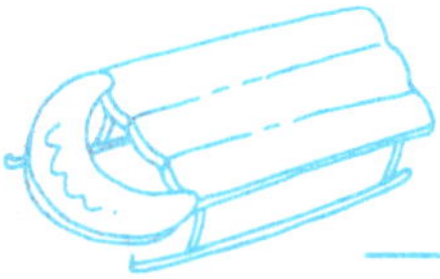

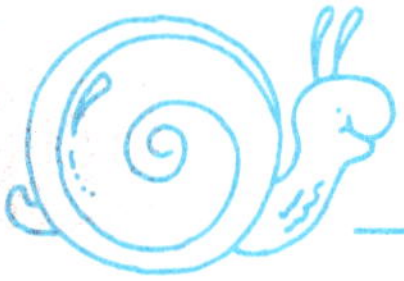

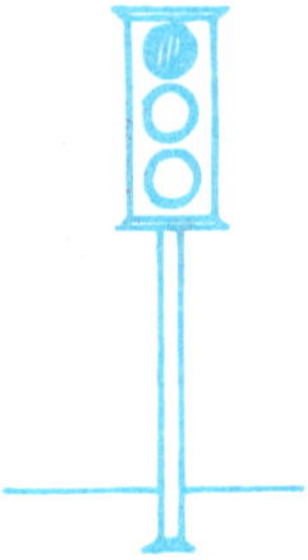

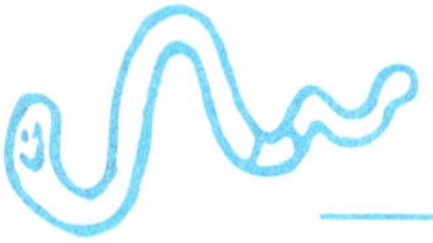

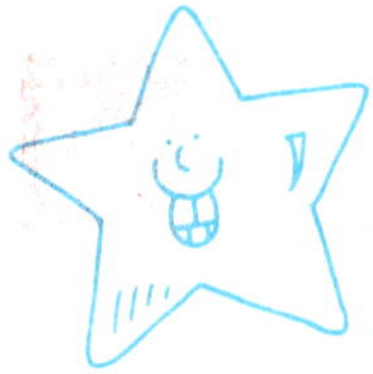

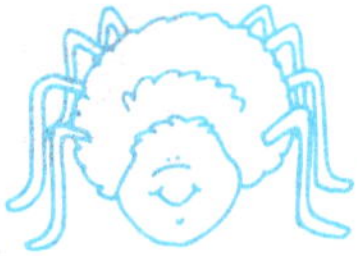

Why don't mountains get cold in the winter?

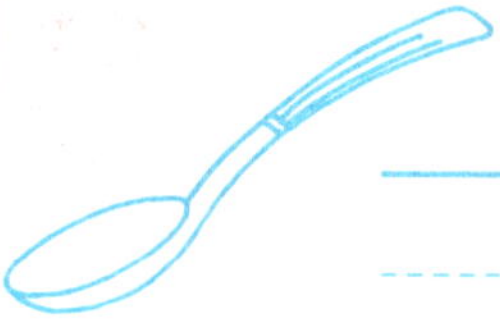

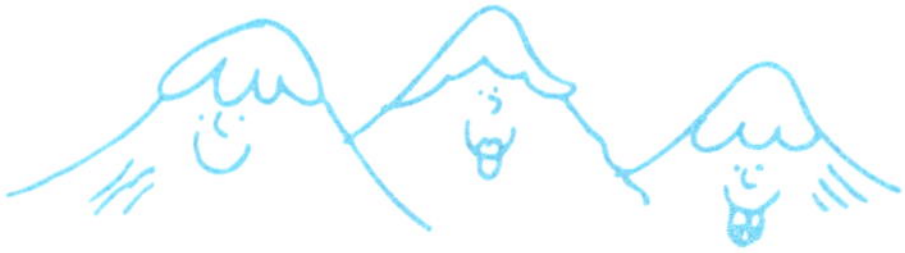

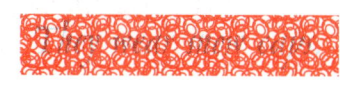

Blends at the End

Final Blends

Look at the first word in each row. Follow the word pattern and fill in the missing letters.

nest	b _____ _____ _____	t _____ _____ _____
pest	r _____ _____ _____	v _____ _____ _____
king	r _____ _____ _____	br _____ _____ _____
sing	st _____ _____ _____	th _____ _____ _____
lamp	r _____ _____ _____	c _____ _____ _____
tent	s _____ _____ _____	l _____ _____ _____

Complete the sentences using words from above.

Birds lay eggs in a _____.

Bees can _____.

Today we will have a spelling _____.

Turn on a _____ so you can see.

Who wears the largest shoes in the world?

_____

You've Got the Hang of This!
Consonant Blends Review

Write the missing blend: bl, cl, fl, gl, pl, or sl.

____ock

____ower

____obe

____oud

____ag

____anet

____ant

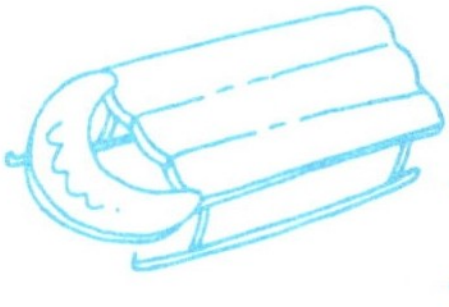

____ed

____ock

____anket

What wears shoes but has no feet?

You're Good at Phonics!
Consonant Blends Review

Circle the letters you hear at the **beginning** of the word.

(cube) bl / cl / gl	(broom) br / tr / pr	(slide) sk / sl / sn
(skate) sk / sl / sn	(clock) cl / fl / gl	(crown) br / pr / cr
(plant) cl / bl / pl	(snail) sk / sw / sn	(flower) bl / cl / fl

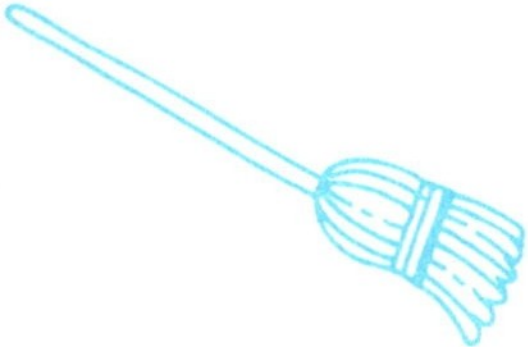

What has one foot on each side and one in the middle?

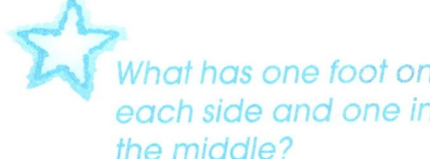

Ever Had a Cherry Shake?
Consonant Digraphs ch, sh

A consonant digraph contains two consonants that appear together in a word. The sound of the digraph is different from the sound of each consonant alone. Write the consonant digraph at the **beginning** of each word.

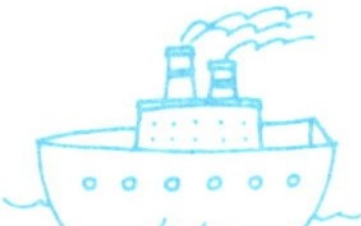

_____ ip

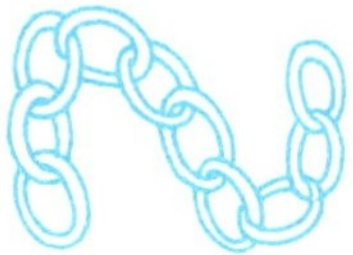

_____ ain

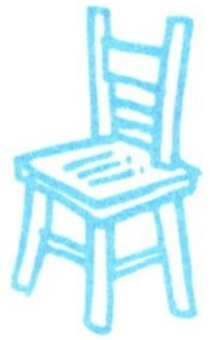

_____ air

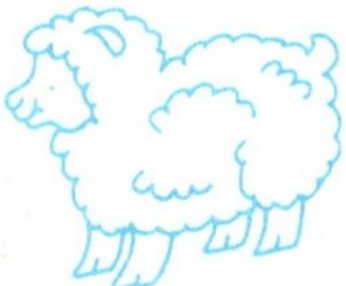

_____ eep

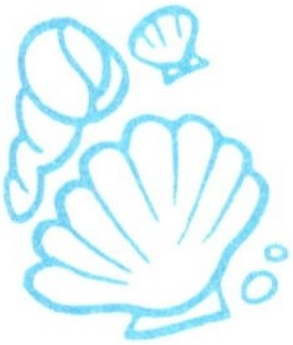

_____ ell

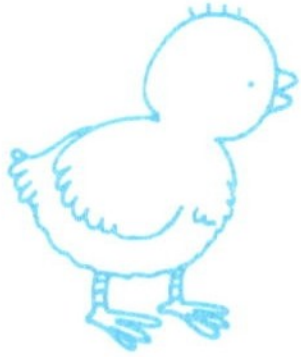

_____ ick

Where do sheep get their hair cut?

The Right Shoe?

Consonant Digraphs sh, th

Write the consonant digraph at the **beginning** of each word.

_____ orn

_____ ark

_____ umb

_____ ip

_____ eep

_____ imble

_____ oe

Why do most people put the right shoe on first?

A Whale of a Good Time

Consonant Digraphs wh, kn

Write the consonant digraph at the **beginning** of each word.

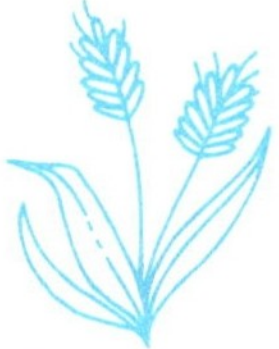

_____ eat

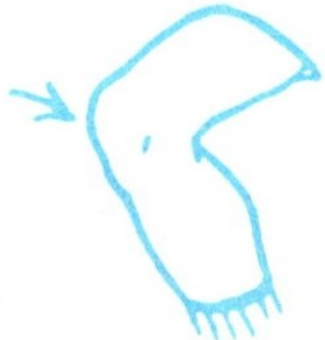

_____ ee

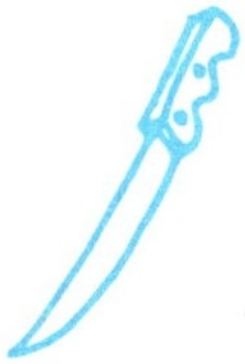

_____ ife

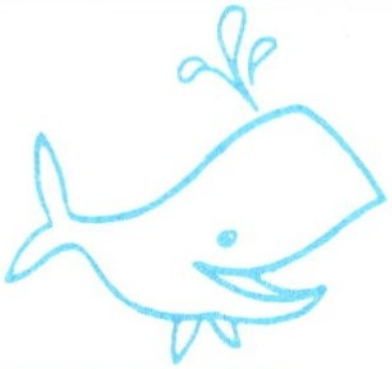

_____ ale

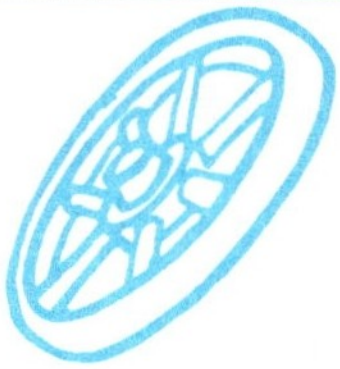

_____ eel

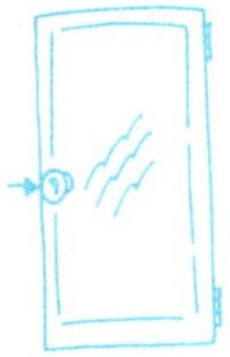

_____ ob

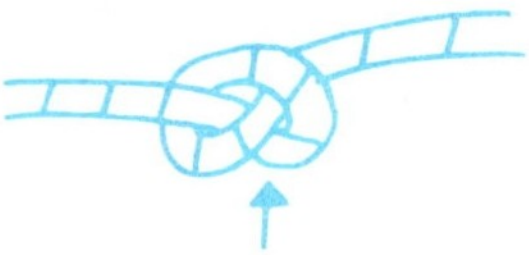

_____ ot

What will happen if you eat yeast and shoe polish at night?

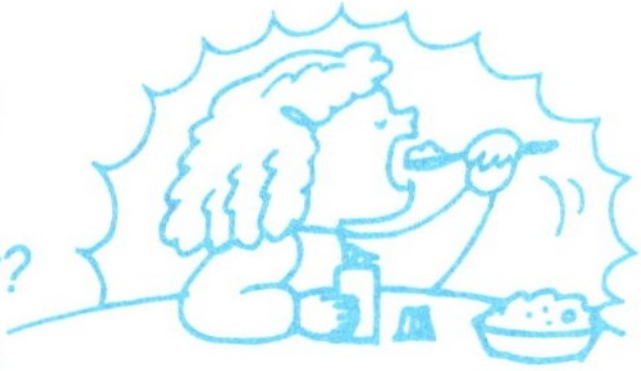

Digraph Footprints

Consonant Digraphs

Print the answers to the riddles. Use the words in the shoe.

wheel   shark
shorts   cherry

I swim in the ocean.

What am I?_____

I am red and round.

What am I?_____

You wear me in summer.

What am I?_____
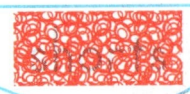

What two-word rhyme describes the mucky stuff on the bottom of your sneakers?

I am round.

What am I?_____

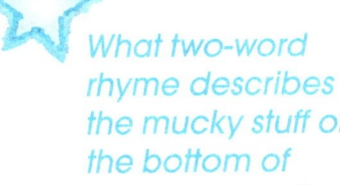

Digraphs at the End
Final Digraphs

Look at the first word in each row. Follow the word pattern and fill in the missing letters.

fish	w _____		d _____	
path	m _____		b _____	
dash	cr _____		tr _____	
hash	s _____		fl _____	
rush	br _____		pl _____	
teach	r _____		b _____	
patch	h _____		b _____	
lunch	b _____		m _____	

What has a tongue but cannot speak?

Take a Photo!

Letter Combination ph

When p and h are together in a word, they may have the sound of the letter f. Circle the ph combination in each word.

telephone   nephew   autograph   alphabet

pheasant   gopher   photo   graph

photograph   telegraph   paragraph   orphan

Fill in the blanks with the correct ph word from the word list.

Did the _____ ring three times this morning?

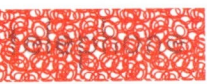

Is the _____ the state animal of Minnesota?

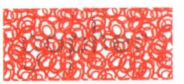

Can you write a _____ about a gopher?

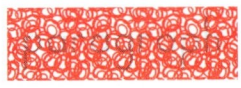

What can't you have until someone else takes it?

© Frank Schaffer Publications, Inc.   FS111119 Phonics Review Grade 2